JPIC Sp Matter
Mattern, Joanne
Do you help others?

$21.00
ocn124031889
10/16/2008

WITHDRAWN

Do You Help Others?/ ¿Ayudas a los demás?

by/por **Joanne Mattern**

Reading consultant/Consultora de lectura: Susan Nations, M.Ed., author/literacy coach/ consultant in literacy development/autora/tutora de alfabetización/ consultora de desarrollo de la lectura

WEEKLY READER®
PUBLISHING

Please visit our web site at: www.garethstevens.com
For a free color catalog describing our list of high-quality books,
call 1-800-542-2595 (USA) or 1-800-387-3178 (Canada).

Library of Congress Cataloging-in-Publication Data

Mattern, Joanne, 1963-
        [Do you help others? Spanish & English]
        Do you help others? = ¿Ayudas a los demás? / by Joanne Mattern.
            p. cm. — (Are you a good friend? = Buenos amigos)
        Includes bibliographical references and index.
        ISBN-10: 0-8368-8283-0 (lib. bdg.)
        ISBN-13: 978-0-8368-8283-4 (lib. bdg.)
        ISBN-10: 0-8368-8288-1 (softcover)
        ISBN-13: 978-0-8368-8288-9 (softcover)
        1. Helping behavior in children--Juvenile literature. 2. Friendship in children—
Juvenile literature. I. Title. II. Title: Ayudas a los demás?
        BF723.H45M3818   2008
        177'.62—dc22   2007018078

First published in 2008 by
Weekly Reader® Books
An imprint of Gareth Stevens Publishing
1 Reader's Digest Road
Pleasantville, NY 10570-7000 USA

Copyright © 2008 by Gareth Stevens, Inc.

Editor: Gini Holland
Art direction: Tammy West
Graphic designer: Dave Kowalski
Picture research: Diane Laska-Swanke
Photographer: Gregg Andersen
Production: Jessica Yanke
Spanish translation: Tatiana Acosta and Guillermo Gutiérrez

Printed in the United States of America

1 2 3 4 5 6 7 8 9 11 10 09 08 07

Note to Educators and Parents

Reading is such an exciting adventure for young children! They are beginning to integrate their oral language skills with written language. To encourage children along the path to early literacy, books must be colorful, engaging, and interesting; they should invite the young reader to explore both the print and the pictures.

The *Are You a Good Friend?* series is designed to help children learn the special social skills they need to make and keep friends in their homes, schools, and communities. The books in this series teach the social skills of listening, sharing, helping others, and taking turns, showing readers how and why these skills help establish and maintain good friendships.

Each book is specially designed to support the young reader in the reading process. The familiar topics are appealing to young children and invite them to read — and reread — again and again. The full-color photographs and enhanced text further support the student during the reading process.

In addition to serving as wonderful picture books in schools, libraries, homes, and other places where children learn to love reading, these books are specifically intended to be read within an instructional guided reading group. This small group setting allows beginning readers to work with a fluent adult model as they make meaning from the text. After children develop fluency with the text and content, the books can be read independently. Children and adults alike will find these books supportive, engaging, and fun!

— Susan Nations, M.Ed., author, literacy coach,
and consultant in literacy development

Nota para los maestros y los padres

¡Leer es una aventura tan emocionante para los niños pequeños! A esta edad están comenzando a integrar su manejo del lenguaje oral con el lenguaje escrito. Para animar a los niños en el camino de a lectura incipiente, los libros deben ser coloridos, estimulantes e interesantes; deben invitar a los jóvenes lectores a explorar la letra impresa y las ilustraciones.

Buenos amigos es una colección diseñada para ayudar a los jóvenes lectores a aprender las destrezas sociales necesarias para hacer y mantener amistades en casa, en la escuela y en la comunidad. Mediante los libros de esta colección, los lectores aprenderán por qué escuchar, compartir, turnarse con los demás y brindar ayuda son destrezas sociales necesarias para establecer y mantener buenas amistades.

Cada libro está especialmente diseñado para ayudar a los jóvenes lectores en el proceso de lectura. Los temas familiares llaman la atención de los niños y los invitan a leer una y otra vez. Las fotografías a todo color y el tamaño de la letra ayudan aún más al estudiante en el proceso de lectura.

Además de servir como maravillosos libros ilustrados en escuelas, bibliotecas, hogares y otros lugares donde los niños aprenden a amar la lectura, estos libros han sido especialmente concebidos para ser leídos en un grupo de lectura guiada. Este contexto permite que los lectores incipientes trabajen con un adulto que domina la lectura mientras van determinando el significado del texto. Una vez que los niños dominan el texto y el contenido, los libros pueden ser leídos de manera independiente. ¡Estos libros les resultarán útiles, estimulantes y divertidos a niños y a adultos por igual!

— Susan Nations, M.Ed., autora/tutora de alfabetización/
consultora de desarrollo de la lectura

Are you a good friend? One way
to be a good friend is to help others.
Do you know how to help others?

- - - - - - - - - - - - - - - - - - - -

¿Eres un buen amigo o una buena
amiga? Algo que hacen los buenos
amigos es ayudar a los demás.
¿Sabes cómo ayudar a los demás?

Helping means doing something for another person. There are many ways to help others. You can help a friend clean up.

Ayudar significa hacer algo por otra persona. Hay muchas maneras de ayudar a los demás. Puedes ayudar a tus amigos a ordenar las cosas.

You can help a friend at school.
It is good to work together!

Puedes ayudar a tus amigos en
la escuela. ¡Trabajar con otra
persona es algo muy bueno!

9

Teaching a friend is a good way of helping. You can teach a friend how to do something new.

- -

Una buena manera de ayudar a tus amigos es **enseñarles** cómo hacer algo. Puedes enseñarles a hacer algo nuevo.

You can help friends outside.
Games are more fun when
friends help each other.

- -

Puedes ayudar a tus amigos
cuando están al aire libre.
Los juegos son más divertidos
cuando los amigos se ayudan
mutuamente.

13

A friend might have a job to do.
You can help.

Quizás alguno de tus amigos tenga
tareas que hacer. Lo puedes ayudar.

The people in your **family** are your first friends. You can help your family by doing **chores** at home.

- -

Los miembros de tu **familia** son tus primeros amigos. Puedes ayudar a tu familia con los **quehaceres domésticos**.

Sometimes, our **neighbors** are our friends. You can help your neighbors with chores, too!

- - - - - - - - - - - - - - - - - - -

A veces, somos amigos de nuestros **vecinos**. ¡También puedes ayudarlos con los quehaceres domésticos!

Friends are happy to help each other. Helping each other can make friends feel good.

- - - - - - - - - - - - - - - - - - - -

A los amigos les encanta ayudarse mutuamente. Ayudar a nuestros amigos hace que nos sintamos bien.

Glossary

chores — jobs

family — a group of people who are related to each other

neighbors — people who live near each other

teaching — showing someone how to do something

Glosario

enseñar — mostrarle a alguien cómo hacer algo

familia — groupo de personas relacionadas

quehaceres domésticos — tareas del hogar

vecinos — personas que viven cerca

For More Information/ Más información

Being Helpful. Janine Amos (Gareth Stevens)

Friendliness. Character Education (series). Lucia Raatma (Bridgestone Books)

I'm Good at Helping. Eileen M. Day (Heinemann Library)

Let's Do It Together. You and Me (series). Denise M. Jordan (Heinemann Library)

Index

Índice

About the Author

Joanne Mattern has written more than 150 books for children. Joanne also works in her local library. She lives in New York State with her husband, three daughters, and assorted pets. She enjoys animals, music, reading, going to baseball games, and visiting schools to talk about her books.

Información sobre la autora

Joanne Mattern ha escrito más de 150 libros para niños. Además, Joanne trabaja en la biblioteca de su comunidad. Vive en el estado de Nueva York con su esposo, sus tres hijas y varias mascotas. A Joanne le gustan los animales, la música, ir al béisbol, leer y hacer visitas a las escuelas para hablar de sus libros.